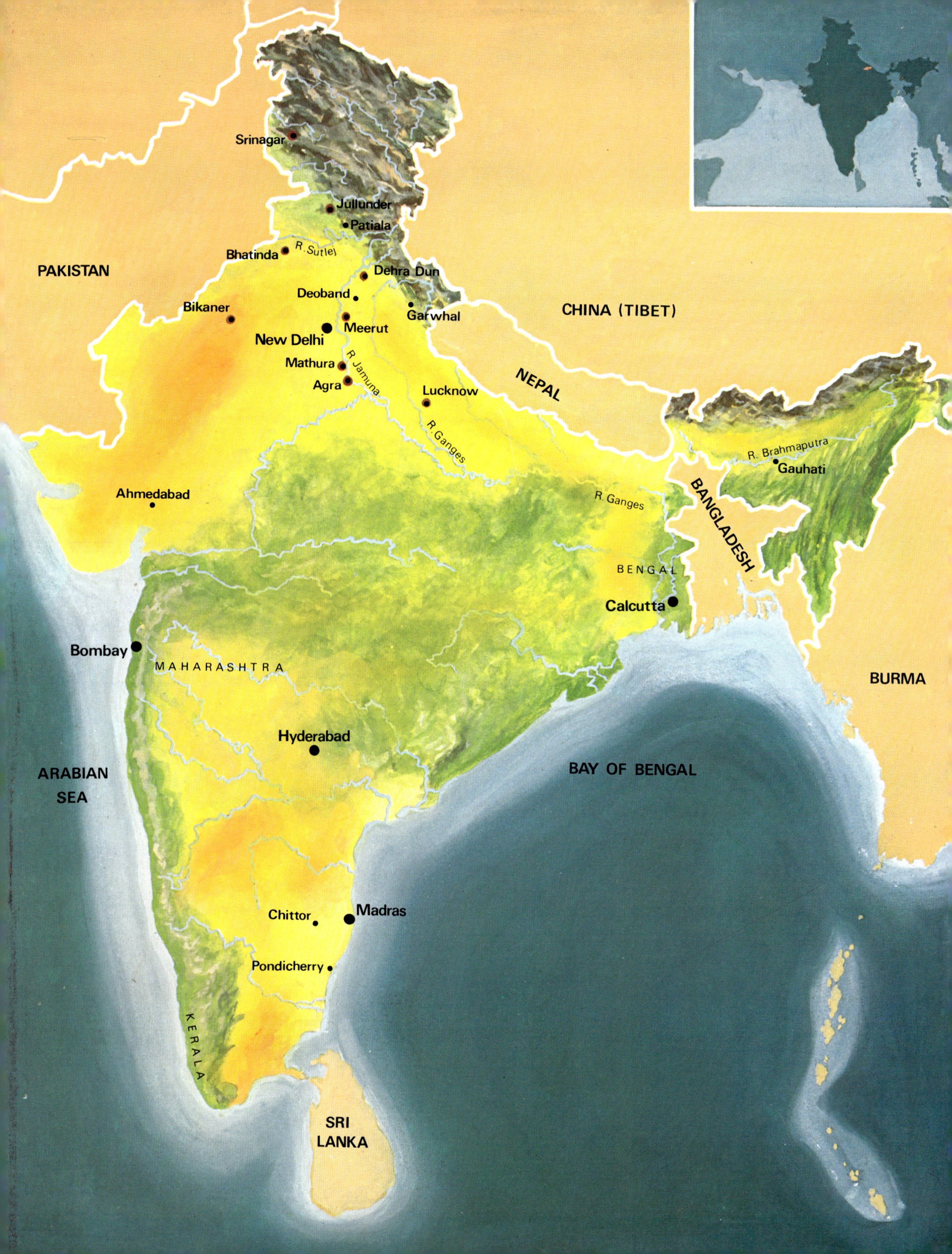

Srinagar
Jullunder
Patiala
Bhatinda
R. Sutlej
PAKISTAN
Dehra Dun
Deoband
Garwhal
Bikaner
Meerut
New Delhi
CHINA (TIBET)
Mathura
R. Jamuna
Agra
Lucknow
NEPAL
R. Ganges
R. Brahmaputra
Gauhati
Ahmedabad
R. Ganges
BANGLADESH
BENGAL
Calcutta
Bombay
MAHARASHTRA
BURMA
Hyderabad
ARABIAN
SEA
BAY OF BENGAL
Chittor
Madras
Pondicherry
KERALA
SRI
LANKA

we live in INDIA

Veenu Sandal

Photography by
Brahm Dev

Wayland

Living Here

We live in Argentina
We live in Australia
We live in Brazil
We live in Britain
We live in Canada
We live in the Caribbean
We live in Chile
We live in China
We live in Denmark
We live in East Germany
We live in France
We live in Greece
We live in Hong Kong
We live in India
We live in Indonesia
We live in Israel
We live in Italy
We live in Japan
We live in Kenya
We live in Malaysia and Singapore
We live in Mexico
We live in the Netherlands
We live in New Zealand
We live in Pakistan
We live in the Philippines
We live in Poland
We live in South Africa
We live in Spain
We live in Sweden
We live in the U.S.A.
We live in the Asian U.S.S.R.
We live in the European U.S.S.R.
We live in West Germany

Further titles are in preparation

First published in 1981 by
Wayland (Publishers) Ltd
49 Lansdowne Place, Hove
East Sussex BN3 1HF, England

Second impression 1985

ISBN 0 85340 858 0

Phototypeset by Trident Graphics Ltd
Reigate, Surrey
Printed in Italy by G. Canale & C.S.p.A., Turin
Bound in the U.K. by The Bath Press

Contents

Ram Swarup, *fruit seller* 6
Shanker Lal Joshi, *camel postman* 8
Raj Kumar **Randir Singh**, *Prince and sportsman* 10
Shivani Das, *student* 12
Maharaj Sing Mathur, *curator of ancient monuments* 14
Sanjay Kaul, *schoolboy* 16
Kamal Singh, *policeman* 18
Pandit **Hardwari Lal**, *priest* 20
V. P. Munusamy, *politician* 22
Madan Mohan Bhatt, *auto-rickshaw driver* 24
Padam Kumar Jain, *scholar* 26
Mohammed Aslam, *industrialist* 28
Abdul Gafoor, *hakim* 30
Asha Kalra, *housewife* 32
Janu Mahdu Kurkutay, *tribal headman* 34
Chowdhry **Narendar Singh**, *farmer* 36
Guru Hanuman, *wrestling coach* 38
Phulki, *blacksmith* 40
Shib Dayal Singh, *zookeeper* 42
Rajinder Nath, *drama director* 44
Ramaswami, *fortune teller* 46
Praveen Sood, *film actor* 48
Dipali Das, *security assistant* 50
Jasbir Singh Kaith, *tailor* 52
Atma Ram, *potter* 54
Salma Sultan, *newsreader* 56
K. Ramakrishnan, *editor* 58
Hira Lal Tayal, *engineer* 60
India Facts 62
Glossary 63
Index 64

'Pavement sellers have to bargain and haggle'

Ram Swarup is a 36-year-old fruit seller in Lucknow, the capital of Uttar Pradesh, India's largest state. He lives with his family in two rented rooms.

Seeing all this fruit may make your mouth water, but for me it's an everyday affair. I've spent the last eighteen years dealing in fruit – so many different varieties, for our country is rich in fruits. In summer, mangoes are the most popular. They're delicious and cheap. A kilo of good variety mangoes sells anywhere between Rs. 3.50 and Rs. 6 (Rs. 1.6 to Rs. 2.7 a pound) when in season.

Then we have lichis, melons, watermelons, apples, oranges, pineapples, papayas, bananas, guavas, plums, coconuts, cherries, raspberries, grapes, loquats, and so many other types of fruit.

My sales are very brisk, as most upper- and middle-class Indians eat fruit at lunch-time. I get up at five every morning and after a quick bath and a cup of tea, walk down to the market to bid for fruit. It's a very busy scene at that time, with each fruit and vegetable dealer trying to shout down the others.

There was a time when all the vegetables and fruits were brought to the market by bullock carts and labourers. Now trucks also help to bring in the produce from farms and orchards.

After I've bought all the fruit I need for the day, I hire a *tonga* to carry the fruit crates to my stall. There are very few air-conditioned vegetables and fruit stores in India. Some do exist in big cities like Bombay, Delhi and Calcutta or Madras and Bangalore. But most towns and villages still have the traditional roadside vegetable and fruit markets.

If you can get your fruit and vegetables fresh, why buy them frozen? Frozen vegetables and fruit lose some of their natural flavour and we Indians are very particular about having just the right flavour in our food.

I and a few others like me own our stalls. Most selling of fruit and vegetables is carried out by pavement sellers or from vegetable and fruit carts. Actually, the four-wheeled carts are a bit of an advantage as one can move around from street to street. But it's some job pushing them in the heat.

Most of us stall owners have fixed

rates. But with pavement sellers and cart wallahs, you have to bargain and haggle.

I earn about Rs. 400 a month, much more than I earned some years ago. But I'm not happy. The cost of living is rising so fast, it makes it very difficult for me to look after my family. Like many other Indians, I'm not in favour of my wife taking a job. But if costs continue to rise at this rate, I may have to ask my wife to make some extra money by knitting or sewing for people.

I'm not educated, so nobody would give me a regular job. Here in India, educational qualifications count for a lot. That's why, even though it's difficult to pay for books and things, I send my children to school. They at least will be able to get good jobs and lead comfortable lives.

From early in the morning till nine at night I'm at my stall, weighing out fruit, watching people pass by, or, perhaps, discussing politics with the neighbouring shopkeepers. Here in India, we're very fond of discussing politics – and of celebrating festivals. *Diwali*, the festival of lights, is my favourite.

Ram Swarup's wife Bimpa grinds flour in the traditional manner.

The price of the vegetables is not marked. Customers have to haggle for their food.

I take a short, one-hour break to go home for lunch. We never have beef, of course. Beef is forbidden in India, as the cow is a holy animal.

Life isn't that bad for me. But I feel sorry for my wife, who has to work even harder than I do at home. She has to cook over a wood fire, even on the hottest of days. Then there's all the cleaning and washing as well. You know, sweeping has to be done with a small broom here in our country, though I've heard that they use something called vacuum cleaners in advanced countries.

Strangely, my wife herself is content. 'Be thankful to God for whatever he has given us,' she tells me. 'You're earning honest money, aren't you? You're not begging or stealing. That's enough for me,' she says.

'Shifting sand dunes change the geography'

Shanker Lal Joshi is a 32-year-old camel postman of Bikaner. He travels in the desert for days at a time. His wife, Parbati Devi, looks after their three-roomed mud dwelling, and their two children.

Every day, people of the Thar Desert in Rajasthan climb the nearest sand dune and look out for me. You see, most of the year round, I'm their only link with the outside world. I bring the desert people news from their near and dear ones, and then carry their news and good wishes back across the desert.

In fact, as I sit on my camel and plod through the sands of the lonely desert, I often marvel at the guts of the desert people. Sometimes, when the rain-water tanks dry up, they have to go without water for days.

Both men and women in the Thar, also known as the Great Indian Desert, spend their lives fighting for survival. They're mainly peasants, and keep herds of cattle, which they sell at annual cattle fairs held on the edge of the desert.

Of course, at times of severe drought, the Army moves in with its vehicles and supplies the desert people with water. But how they and their cattle manage to live throughout the year remains a mystery to me, for you can't see a blade of grass in hundreds of square miles.

The desert is no place to live or move, I often tell myself when I'm loading my camel with the post. A camel post office certainly is unusual. Ever since the first post office was set up in Calcutta in 1774, the Posts and Telegraph Department has been determined to put every little place in India on the postal map.

There are 125,283 post offices in India with about 731,716 workers. Of these offices, 26,062 are mobile rural post

Desert people come out to meet their postman, often their only link with the outside world.

offices, and yet there are quite a few areas which remain without postal services.

Before the mobile camel post office was started in 1974, the desert people had to walk miles and miles to send news, and then wait months and months to receive answers to their letters. It wasn't possible to have a regular postal service, as shifting sand dunes keep changing the geography of the area. But our camel post office has solved the problem for both the people and the postal department.

But mark you, my life as a camel postman is far from easy. Searing winds and blinding sand storms screech across the Thar. The wind and the sand make such an awful moaning noise, I sometimes have to pray in the middle of the desert. I and my camel are out there all alone, you see. It's such a relief to see some deer or black bucks or bustards – they're fairly common in the desert here.

Quite often, I come across the skeletons of cattle and people who have died of thirst because they lost their way. It's easy to lose one's way, with the sand dunes shifting from one place to another. I know that if something were ever to happen to my camel, we would both probably die, for help always comes too late in the desert. So I'm very grateful to my camel for taking me and the mail safely across the sands, from one hut to another.

We have about twenty-two camel postmen. The post office pays me Rs. 100 a month, and Rs. 20 for my camel. But then, besides the mail box, I and other camel postmen are allowed to carry private goods from place to place. Two of my brothers are also camel postmen. In the rainy season, all three of us work as part-time agricultural labourers.

A colourful sight in a colourful region: Barmer dancers dressed as bridegrooms.

The government has started this Rajasthan Canal Scheme under which they're bringing water to more and more of the desert. Ultimately, they hope to make the entire desert green, but it will take a lot of time, I feel.

When I'm on the move, I have difficulty getting food. So my wife gives me several days supply of thick, sweetened *rotis* baked on slabs of stone. Fortunately, my wife and children stay the whole year round at Bikaner, where everything is available.

Leading the life that I do, there's barely time for relaxation. But at harvest time, folk dancers make us forget our life of labour. To outsiders, of course, our area has a lot to offer – colourful dresses, women laden with silver jewellery, and camel safaris. But I for one wouldn't recommend the desert to anyone.

'I shot my first tiger when I was fourteen'

***Raj Kumar* Randhir Singh of Patiala is a 35-year-old sportsman. With his wife and two daughters he lives in a nine-roomed house with eight servants and three cars.**

People who don't know me are startled when they see me armed with my gun. But then they don't know that I spend a lot of time simply practising shooting. I've participated in the shooting events in five Olympics so far. And I've won medals in the Bavarian Championships in Germany, at the Commonwealth Games, and in the Asian Games. But I'm still chasing an Olympic medal.

It's quite a busy life for me, for besides practising shooting, I have to look after my business and farms. I earn a very comfortable income, and I spend lavishly too.

You see, as a *Raj Kumar* of the royal family of Patiala, I have to keep up my position. My father is a *rajah*. But mind you, these days, we're *nawabs* and *rajahs* only in our names and styles of living.

Of course, we still own land and property, and some royal families still live in their palaces and keep elephants and tigers. But there's no comparison with the pomp and glamour and huge estates of, say, forty years ago.

We're no longer a privileged lot, you see. We have to take up occupations and move around just as other people do. Of course, on occasions, we have to dress regally in rich silks and satins and gold brocade. And it's nice to know that people respect us.

The Prince stands with his wife, Uma Kumari, and his dog, Rusty.

Mementoes of the past: big game hunting has been banned in India for some years.

Perhaps this is the reason why a number of us from the royal families have decided to serve the people by seeking election for Parliament. Why, at present, there are three Members of Parliament from my own Patiala family.

We're also campaigning very hard for the improvement of sports in the country. We've all been great sportsmen you know. My great grandfather, Maharaja Rajinder Singh, supported some of the finest wrestlers and cricketers of his time. In fact, the Indian Olympic Association was founded by my grandfather, Maharaja Bhupendra Singh.

Times have changed, as you know. We no longer have the money to support entire sports teams. But we are striving for better training and living conditions for our country's sportsmen. We're a poor country, true, and food and population control must get first priority. But how, I keep asking the government, can you expect your sportsmen to do well if you don't take the trouble to provide them with modern equipment?

Even with my campaigning, my shooting and my business, I do get some spare time. When I was very young, it was usual to go hunting. I shot my first tiger when I was just fourteen years old and shot two more later on.

It was all very exciting, but now I've become conscious of preserving wildlife. So I only go boar hunting or on partridge shoots.

One can still go hunting in India, but only for deer and smaller animals and birds. Big game hunting was banned a few years ago, unless, of course, there's a man-eating tiger at large.

We are firm believers in God. Every morning, my wife and I spend an hour praying. I'm a Sikh, so we read out aloud from the *Granth Sahib*, the religious book of all Sikhs, like the Christian Bible. Our family also worships Durga, the Goddess who rides on a tiger.

'We young people should be allowed more freedom'

Shivani Das is an 18-year-old college student of Bengal, specializing in Indian history. She lives with her parents.

I study in a co-educational college. In two years time, I hope to pass my examinations and become a graduate with a Bachelor of Arts Degree. We now have 118 universities in India compared with just forty-seven twenty years ago. We also have more than 4,569 colleges and over 2 million college students.

Most colleges, particularly in smaller towns and even in cities, are either girls' colleges or boys' colleges. In fact, co-education in our country came into fashion only with the British. And a good thing too.

But we young ones in India still have a number of problems. Since Independence, our country has made a lot of progress. Yet socially, so many problems remain to be solved. For example, boys here are pampered and considered valuable as they're the moneymakers. You see, when they grow up, not only do they bring in money from jobs, but they also fetch huge dowries in large parts of the country. In fact, women who have only daughters and no sons are quite often looked down upon by their mothers-in-law.

You know, there's an old saying here in India – 'old is gold'. Look at our politicians. They're generally in their 60s, 70s and 80s, and don't want to retire and give up their place to the younger generation.

Most young people here don't get regular pocket money. Nor can we from the upper and middle classes take up part-time jobs as in some Western countries. This means that, till we become graduates and take up jobs or start our own businesses, we have to depend upon our parents for everything.

In fact, it's not considered respectable for a young person to protest or disagree with one's elders. And since we don't have any financial independence, we have to do what our parents tell us to do. Honestly, I feel we young people should be allowed more freedom.

Life is so different for the young from poor families. Few poor youngsters reach college. To help their families, they have

Girls and boys can't mix freely in India, but co-education helps to relax traditional tabus.

to take up whatever work they can find, often when they're just seven or eight years old, as newspaper or shoeshine boys, or servants, or ice-cream vendors. Or they become beggars. People say: 'Oh, look at all those beggars on the roadside – it's terrible.' But then they don't realize how very difficult life can be here in India.

No man in India would want to marry a girl who has had an 'affair', as they call it. And as for a girl inviting a boy home or a boy inviting a girl home, merely for a friendly chat, it's just not done in most homes. So you see, girls and boys can't really mix freely. My parents are pretty broad-minded, but even they wouldn't approve if I began dating or if my boy-friends began dropping in at home as my girl friends do.

I've been complaining a lot, but you know, if we young ones keep quiet, we'll never change anything. Of course, we have good customs too. We look after our parents in their old age. A lot of Indian homes also give a weekly contribution to the poor.

Not all learning comes from books. Here a college girl studies village art.

'We've got about 5000 ancient monuments'

Maharaj Singh Mathur, 52, is a curator of monuments. He and his wife, Sheela, live in Agra, the city of the Taj Mahal.

My job is to look after the monuments of India; we've got about 5,000 of them. A large number are really ancient, dating back to the first century B.C.

It's quite amazing that our people of so long ago could build such fantastic structures which have lasted for thousands of years. They didn't have the modern tools and machines that we do. They had to build mainly by hand.

I haven't visited all the monuments in India. They're scattered all over the country for one thing. Besides, it's not really possible to visit all 5,000 or so of them. But I've visited the more important and interesting ones and those which needed my attention – about 400 in all.

You see, I've been allotted a certain area. Within that area, I have to see that the monuments remain in good shape. Some of them are so old that carrying out repairs is quite a job. We have to go searching for the same stone or marble that was used long ago.

The Taj Mahal, of course, is the greatest of our monuments. It's still one of the Wonders of the World. Foreign tourists who come to India don't want to go away without seeing the Taj Mahal, especially by moonlight.

Ancient temple sculptures such as these must be protected from the effects of pollution.

The Jantar Mantar is a centuries-old observatory and monument to India's past.

It was built by the Mughal Emperor Shah Jahan for his beloved wife, Mumtaz Mahal. It's too beautiful for words.

But like a lot of other monuments in India, it's in danger now – from industrial pollution. As more and more factories and refineries are going up in the country, preserving the precious monuments from their smoke and other chemicals is becoming quite a task. So I and others in the Archaeological Department are studying new ways of preserving them.

The Sun Temple at Konarak is wonderful. It's full of sculpted figures. The Jagannath Temple in Orissa is also very famous, as are the mountain monasteries in Ladakh, and some of our cave temples like Ajanta, Ellora and Elephanta Caves.

Compared with twenty years ago, I've noticed that people don't want to work hard. They look for the easy way. Some time ago, I had to walk sixty-one kilometres (38 miles) in a day, through the jungle, to reach a monument. And I didn't mind. But today, if I were to ask one of my staff to walk thirty-eight miles, they would say: 'Aw! Isn't there any other way?'

So modern comforts have been good, but they've made us soft. Then there's this awful dowry system. It's worse now than it was twenty years ago. I've seen people with three or four daughters being ruined by it. I'm lucky that in my caste there is no dowry system.

When I'm off duty, I read, or take my wife and children to a movie or to some party. Sometimes we go to a function; we attended a name-giving ceremony the other day. All Hindu names have a meaning. My name is Maharaj, which means 'a lord'. My wife's name Sheela means 'a good character'. My son's name Sunil means 'a red lotus', and so on.

'We have floating gardens and market places'

Sanjay Kaul is a 17-year-old schoolboy in Srinagar, the capital of Kashmir, India's northernmost state.

I'm in my last year at school and studying very hard to obtain good results in my examinations. I know that getting a job will depend on whether I get good marks or not.

I go to a Western-type co-educational public school. Such schools are very expensive and only about a quarter of India's children attend them; the rest go to schools where lessons are in Hindi. I'm at school from seven in the morning to one in the afternoon in summer, and from nine in the morning to three in the afternoon in winter.

My uniform is trousers, and a shirt and tie, with a blazer in winter. The girls wear skirts, blouses and a tie. But in the village schools and most Hindi-language schools, where there are more boys than girls, the boys wear Indian dress, like pyjamakurta.

In the rural areas, most schools follow the ancient Indian pattern of education. Classes are held in the open under the shade of trees, and they teach a very high level of Sanskrit.

The fair-skinned beauty of Kashmiri women is legendary throughout India.

There are around 517,250 schools in India. My father tells me that the number of schools today is more than three times the number that existed twenty years ago. To fight illiteracy, the government has made primary education compulsory and free in most states.

Our school has recently taken us on several study tours. Each time we visited a different part of India it seemed we were visiting a new land. The language, the food, the clothes were all so different. There was such a big gap between the rich and the poor. I could never imagine that the poor could be so very poor. Seeing all this disturbed me a lot.

But no part of India compares with my homeland. Kashmir is a green valley full of lakes and rivers and meadows, lying high in the Himalayas – the world's highest mountains. Srinagar, the capital, is known as the 'Venice of the East', because there are more waterways here than roads, with dozens of houseboats and smaller boats known as *doongas*. We even have a floating post office and floating gardens and market-places. The *hangis* (boat people) of Kashmir perform their weddings on the water, in their boats. We also have the world's highest golf course and one of the world's highest mines – it produces sapphires.

People from other parts of India often say that we Kashmiris are always on holiday. That's because our valley has everything – cool weather, skiing, mountaineering, fishing, speedboat racing, and beautiful women and handsome men. Actually, we Kashmiris are more Persian than Indian in appearance. I'm a Hindu, but the population of Kashmir are largely Moslem. Our handicrafts are famous – silks, rich hand-woven carpets, sweet-smelling cedar-wood trays and boxes.

I haven't yet decided upon a particular career, mainly because I'm interested in many subjects. We're taught so many in school – English, Hindi, Sanskrit, geography, history, civics, moral science, botany, arithmetic, algebra, geometry, physics, chemistry. Hindi and English are compulsory, and we have to choose another four.

With more waterways than roads in Srinagar, houseboats are an obvious choice of home.

'One of the most powerful gangs is led by a woman'

Kamal Singh is a 29-year-old police constable of Meerut. His ambition is to become a police inspector.

When I joined the police force five years ago, I thought patrolling the streets and directing traffic was all there was to the job. Now I know how tough and dangerous a policeman's life can really be.

Sometimes we have to chase armed *dacoits* (robbers) or pick-pockets, or break up a fight between hoodlums, or lay a trap for thieves. Other times we have to check whether a bullock cart is overloaded, because cruelty to animals is an offence in our country. Sometimes we have to guard a prisoner or give evidence in the courts. We also have to accompany processions, which are frequent in India, to ensure law and order.

I don't carry arms unless I'm on a special mission. Normally I only have a *lathi* (a long wooden baton). To break up a crowd we make a '*lathi* charge'. But

Cruelty to animals is an offence, so police check that bullock carts are not overloaded.

usually our uniform alone is enough to scare away trouble makers.

The other evening I set off on a routine patrol with five other policemen, carrying our *lathis* and powerful torches. All was peaceful, until around half-past eight we rounded a bend in the river and ran straight into a group of people. We didn't know they were thieves, and because it was dark, they didn't know at first that we were policemen.

But when we challenged them and they realized who we were, they fired at us. We threw ourselves to the ground and fortunately, perhaps because it was dark, none of us got hit. Seeing their chance, the thieves made a dash for it, but I was able to give chase and catch one of them.

Guess what they had been stealing. Roadside electric wires, of all things. They had a long stick with a sharp blade on the end with which they cut the wires. We recovered 40 kilograms (88 lb) of wire from them. And I received a cash award for catching one of the thieves.

Life here is becoming safer each year. That's mainly because our police force is now equipped with modern aids like radios, radar, automatic weapons, dog squads and experts; this makes it easier to trace the culprits.

We're trying our best to wipe out the dreaded *dacoits* of the Chambal Valley. The area, with its ravines, rivers and jungles, has long been famous for its bandits. There are more than a hundred *dacoits* of different gangs operating there. They attack and loot mainly the rich or people who have informed on them. One of the most powerful gangs has a horse-riding, rifle-carrying woman as the leader. She is known as *Phoolan Devi*, the Queen of Bandits. There are several women *dacoits* in the area. All of them are crack shots.

All Indian kutcheries *or law courts have large shady trees under which people can work.*

I think that here in India poverty and unemployment are the two main causes of crime. There are over 8.4 million unemployed in the country. If everybody had enough to eat and work to occcupy them, there would be fewer crimes. Of course, we're fortunate not to have Mafia-type connections or organizations.

My salary of Rs. 500 a month is enough for me and my family. We spend it mainly on food and clothes. Most days we eat *chapatis, dal,* and lots of cooked vegetables like mashed aubergines, pumpkins, tomatoes and lady's fingers. I'm quite particular about eating food with a spoon, but most people still eat the traditional Indian way – with their hands. We speak Hindi at home, but I can also speak English and understand Punjabi and Garhwali.

'We Hindu people have thousands of gods'

***Pandit* Hardwari Lal is a 55-year-old priest. He works more than fifteen hours a day at his temple in Bhatinda.**

My day at the temple begins at half-past four in the morning and ends at eight o'clock every night. It's a long day, but I don't mind one bit, as I devote all the time to the service of God.

Which God, you ask? Well, we Hindus have 330 million deities. We believe that the God Brahma is the Creator of the World. Vishnu is the God who preserves the world and the God Shiva is the destroyer of the world.

Among the more popular gods and goddesses are Radha and Krishna, Ram and Sita, Hanuman the monkey God, Ganesha the elephant-headed God, and the Goddess Durga, who rides a tiger. We have lots of idols of these gods and goddesses in our temple. You'll find lots of temples, at least one every mile or so in India, for religion is very important here.

It's part of my duty as a priest to offer prayer to the idols, to bathe them with milk and honey, and to dress them. Then, every day, I and other temple priests have to organize the distribution of free food. Our temple feeds about thirty or forty poor people every day. The temple gets its money from donations.

Only a Brahman can become a priest in a temple. He must be learned in the

At Hindu wedding ceremonies, not only the brides dress for the occasion.

ancient Sanskrit texts known as *Vedas*. He must also know how to conduct weddings, birth and death ceremonies and so on.

Most marriages are finally arranged after comparing the horoscopes of the boy and girl. If the astrologer feels that they will get along, he fixes an auspicious day and hour for the wedding. Last year, for almost eight months, practically no weddings took place, as the stars weren't in the right position.

Anyhow, on the chosen day, the bridegroom dresses in style with a shining crown on his head and garlands of flowers and bank-notes round his neck. He then sits on a white horse – though some people prefer motor-cars nowadays. Escorted by a band of drummers and trumpeters and a whole lot of relatives and friends, the groom goes through the streets to the bride's place. The bride has to wear lots of jewellery and dress in red or pink.

The priests light the sacred fire of sandalwood and incense and begin reciting *mantras* from the *Vedas*. Then we take a pink cloth and tie one end to the bridegroom and the other end to the bride. The bride and bridegroom have to walk round the sacred fire seven times to become husband and wife. For tens of centuries, Hindu weddings have been performed in the same way.

As for funerals, we Hindus usually burn our dead, though we bury infants.

There are so many holy cities and places. They're usually on the banks of rivers or up on the snowy mountains. Cities like Hardwar, Rishikesh and Varanasi are on the riverside. Pilgrimage centres like Badrinath, Kedarnath and Amarnath are high up in the mountains. Half the year the pilgrims can't get to them because of the snow.

But I must tell you about the Kumbh *Mela*, which is held every twelve years and is the world's greatest religious fair. At Kumbh, millions and millions of Hindus gather from all over India to take a bath in the holy Ganges.

With so much going on, life remains busy and full for me. I can't tell you how happy and fortunate I feel serving God and the people.

The idol of Ganesh, the elephant-faced god.

'70 per cent of our people can't read or write'

V. P. Munusamy is a 48-year-old politician in Pondicherry, where the French ruled for 250 years, till 1954. His wife, Indira, is also a politician. Mr. and Mrs. Munusamy share their time between their home in Pondicherry, and the Parliament at New Delhi.

I'm proud to be a citizen of India, the world's largest democracy. And very happy to be able to serve my country as a Member of Parliament.

Elections are held every five years in India. Our Parliament consists of two houses. The Rajya Sabha, or Council of States, has 244 members. And the Lok Sabha, or the House of the People, has 525 members, directly elected by the people. I myself am a Member of the Rajya Sabha.

I've been in politics for twenty-eight years now. I've spent this time moving around the countryside, meeting people and listening to their problems. Doing this hasn't been easy, mainly because of the language difficulty. I speak only English, Tamil and French, and in the north, where our Parliament sits in New Delhi, they speak a lot in Hindi, which I can't understand. Indeed, I find that India's a very mixed-up country.

We gained independence from the British in 1947. Since that time, there has been tremendous progress in every field. We're among the top ten industrial nations of the world. Our exports alone are worth over Rs. 750 million a year. And we've nuclear power, strictly for peaceful purposes, of course. We've also succeeded in putting two satellites into space. These are fantastic developments.

But I can't really boast, for despite all this, 70 per cent of our people remain poor and can't read or write. In fact, poverty, illiteracy and the population explosion are big, big problems for India.

But age-old beliefs, customs and superstitions stand in our way. People listen to our ideas and say: 'Yes, they're good.' But then they go and do things in the old way and say: 'This has been the way for centuries; why change it now?'

Take the case of the untouchables and the caste system. Over the years the government has been giving every opportunity to the lower classes, but the system is still very much there. The lower classes were named Harijans, meaning Children of God, by Mahatma Gandhi. But nobody treats them as Children of God.

Even at election time, most people vote according to caste. A Brahman will prefer to vote for a Brahman, a Rajput for a Rajput and so on. There are a large number of political parties in India. Since Independence, the Congress Party has remained the largest.

People in our country may not be able to read or write, but they're all very interested in politics. So politicians must try to bring about change. First, we have to persuade people to have smaller families. Otherwise, India will go on doubling its food and goods production, but this will never be enough if the population goes on increasing. As it is, our population is over 660 million.

I myself am a Harijan. When I married my wife, who is a Brahman, there was a big uproar. We had to be brave and face society. It was then that I realized that laws alone won't help. The people themselves must change their ideas and work for progress.

Sunset at Pondicherry, where Mr and Mrs Munusamy live when they are not in Delhi.

Despite the long discussions at election meetings, most Indians vote according to caste.

'Cows are considered holy in India'

Madan Mohan Bhatt, 34, is an auto-rickshaw driver of Garwhal. At harvest time, Madan's wife returns to his parents' village in the mountains to help in the fields.

I began my job as an auto-rickshaw driver twelve years ago. I didn't have much money, so the bank bought an auto-rickshaw for me. I worked off the investment in five years, and now I am the proud owner of my three-wheeled auto-rickshaw.

Life isn't easy for me. For one thing, driving in India is a big strain. Traffic in the large cities, like Delhi and Bombay, is fairly well-regulated, with traffic signals and different lanes. But in most towns these don't exist. And the pedestrians treat the roads as if they were their own.

It took Madan Mohan five years to pay off the loan he needed for his auto-rickshaw.

Then there's the problem of stray cows. Cows are considered holy in India, so even if they sit in the middle of the road, few people are willing to disturb them.

Bullock carts are still the main form of transport for about 70 per cent of the population and I think they're becoming even more popular.

The rich and sometimes the middle class travel around by plane or in air-conditioned buses or train compartments, or taxis. For those who have less money, there are ordinary buses, collective taxis or second-class train carriages. Our railway system is the largest in Asia and the fourth largest in the world: over 10,800 trains run daily.

Twenty years ago there were many carts and cycle rickshaws in our cities,

The Garhwal region is proud of its mountainous beauty.

but auto-rickshaws were rare. Nowadays, they're very common and people in a hurry prefer to hire one – buses are too crowded and don't run on time, and taxis are too expensive and are considered unsafe for women travelling alone.

Summer months and monsoons are the best seasons for my trade: few people want to walk in the hot sun or in the rain on muddy roads. I currently earn about Rs. 40 a day. I used to earn much more but the petrol crisis has hit us. *Tongas* and cycle rickshaws, which were out of fashion, are now coming back. There are around 2.1 million motor vehicles in India, nearly ten times the number there were thirty years ago.

The first thing I do on getting up is to fold my hands and to say *namaskar* to the sun, as I believe in the Sun God. Then, after a breakfast which my wife prepares for me, I leave home at nine and head for the railway station. I can be sure of getting fares there. I speak only Garhwali. Hindi and a bit of English. So it can be quite funny when a person from another part of the country comes up to me. We can't understand each other and have to use hand gestures.

I take a siesta in my rickshaw from two till four in the afternoon. It's terribly hot at that time in the summer, and few people go out. For lunch, I buy something from a roadside cart; I have dinner at a small restaurant.

I wait for fares from the last film show and return home around midnight. My late hours used to upset my wife, but now she realizes that I'm fighting to beat the rising costs.

'Our civilization dates back to 3000 B.C.'

Padam Kumar Jain is a 63-year-old scholar in Agra. He has collected around 20,000 valuable books on India. His wife, Pushpa Mala, runs a primary school. They live in a 12-roomed bungalow.

Ever since I was a boy I've been interested in the culture and people of my land. India is a vast country with many different kinds of people, religions, customs and even weather conditions. How could I get to know about each and all of them? The best way, I thought, would be by reading.

I began collecting books on India and its people. On average, a book cost just six pence in those days. Now, books have become really expensive. But I've been able to collect about 20,000 and a whole lot of journals.

Every year, I'm able to add about 500 new books to my collection. I would like to add more, but that's all I can afford on my monthly income of Rs. 3,500.

Research scholars from all over the country come to use my library. I don't charge them anything for using it.

I'm happy to find that once again our educated young are turning to their own Indian culture. It's very rich and varied.

Our Indus Valley civilization, which dates back to the year 3000 B.C., is one of the oldest civilizations in the world. Scholars and archaeologists from all over the world still come to study the mystery of its ruins.

Soon after the Indus Valley civilization, the fair-skinned Aryan race invaded India. They settled in the north and

The Taj Mahal was built outside Agra by the emperor Shah Jahan in memory of his wife.

drove the old inhabitants of India, the dark-skinned Dravidians, to the south. Much later, both the races mingled together, but the Aryans remained the masters.

It was the Aryans who divided our society into four groups. The Brahmans were considered to be the élite. Then came the warrior class; then the merchants and traders. Butchers, sweepers, and the menial workers were placed in the lowest class and were supposed to be impure and, therefore, untouchable.

So the caste system in India is thousands of years old. Although the educated are now trying to destroy it, it still exists. Happily, this caste system is weakening. In the urban areas, at least, you'll find sweepers' children going to school along with Brahman children. And there are inter-caste marriages, too.

Centuries after the Aryans settled in India, the Moslems began invading. In the sixteenth century, the Moslem Mughals founded a great dynasty and ruled over us for a few hundred years.

Padam Kumar Jain lives with his wife, Pushp Mala, in this twelve-roomed bungalow.

Then the British arrived and became the masters. So India is a mixture of many cultures rolled into one: Hindu culture of the Aryans, Moslem culture, and some British habits. And different religions, of course.

I'm a Jain, but I'm not very religious. I don't eat before sunset or tie a cloth over my nose or keep away from onions and garlic as some religious-minded Jains do. But I and my family follow the Jain practice of not eating meat.

We believe that all life is sacred and that one should not kill either humans or animals. We also don't turn away a poor or hungry person from our door. This, again, is an old Indian tradition.

My own life is simple. I read most of the day – about thirty to forty books a month. Except for lunch with my wife at one o'clock when she returns from school, I have no fixed eating hours.

'We have a plentiful supply of cheap labour'

Mohammed Aslam is a 34-year-old industrialist and exporter. His family and his brother's family share a large bungalow in the Doon Valley. They have 3 servants, 2 cars and 2 motorcycles.

Life's been good to me. I started this factory six years ago, producing hand tools like bench vices. Today, I also make brassware like door-knobs and name-plates. And there's scope to do much more.

I earn about Rs. 5,000 a month. My factory is small compared with the giant industrial complexes at Rourkela and Bhilai. I export my products to the United States, Canada, Germany, Sweden, Australia and the Middle East.

In the last twenty years, our country has advanced tremendously. We are among the top ten industrial nations of the world and we're well on the way to being self-sufficient in making sophisticated machines and gadgets.

We've got our own car factories; and we're making our own aircraft, trains, ships, teleprinters, watches, scooters, motorcycles, drugs, engineering and steel goods. Of course, the cotton textile industry is still the largest single industry in India. There are over 15 million industrial workers in the country.

Still, I do feel that we could double production if we learnt some discipline. At my own factory, where I employ about fifty workers, I find that they're very lazy. They're supposed to work an eight-hour day but they put in only four hours of actual work. They seem to like taking things easy. Perhaps our hot climate has something to do with it. Most people I've met have the same complaint. But then, unlike other countries, we have a plentiful supply of cheap labour.

Another thing that disturbs me: nothing moves here in our country unless you pay a bribe or are related to a high-ranking official. It's become so much a part of our lives that we don't give it a second thought. Of course, it's wrong; but what can one do? When I began my business, I wanted to change things. But like others before me, I soon found that if you didn't pay the extra money and tips, you couldn't get licences, permits or raw materials.

Sometimes I find that life here is too

complex. In one place you'll find very modern people: they've been around the world; they're very liberal, very Westernized. You travel just twenty miles to another place and you'll find people who've never seen a railway engine or a camera. One end you'll find discotheques and jean-clad girls dancing the tango; the other end you'll find ladies who stay in purdah and never leave the house except, perhaps, to fetch water from the well. India is a land full of contrasts.

My day begins with a heavy breakfast of milk, honey, toast and eggs. At nine, I drive the ten miles to my factory. I come back home for lunch at one o'clock. It's a long way to come, I know, but then I love food.

For lunch we usually have rice and some mutton. We rarely eat chapatis, but we take lots of fruit. Dinner is much the same with a different dish of mutton or chicken.

A businessman's time is precious, but Mr Aslam can always find time for his children.

Life for the wealthy is rarely dull. Polo has long been a favourite pastime of the upper classes.

By half-past two I'm back at the factory, where I make plans and discuss details with my foreman. My day ends at four o'clock. Then I rush to the squash courts and play for an hour or two.

I used to be fond of big-game shooting and I bagged four panthers besides deer and other animals. But now I've become aware of wildlife preservation and shoot only birds for the table. I'm still crazy about motorcycles, though, and love breaking speed records.

'I have no modern equipment, not even a thermometer'

Abdul Gafoor is a 96-year-old bonesetter and *hakim* (traditional medicine man). His four sons and their families live with him in a three-roomed house in Deoband.

It's eighty years now since I learnt the skill of setting broken bones and healing people. I don't use anaesthesia, I don't use modern medicine, and I don't have any modern equipment, not even a thermometer.

Actually, a large number of people in India, especially in the villages, make use of ancient Indian systems of medicine like *ayurveda* and *unani*. In fact, *ayurveda* means the 'science of life'. Most villagers and even town and city folk consult hereditary *hakims* and *vaidyas* like me who practise medicine as a family profession.

There are about 300,000 of us in India. There are plenty of modern doctors, too, but not enough. Only one doctor for every 4,200 people. But with 131 medical colleges in the country, things are improving, they tell me.

I myself am the eighth *hakim* in my family. Of course, in the beginning, medicine was not a full time job with me. For forty-eight years, I worked in the law courts, from 10 a.m. to 5 p.m. I used to practise medicine in the evenings only. But now patients come to me throughout the day. Generally, they're dislocation and fracture cases. But also those who are running a fever, suffering pain or some stomach disorder.

Abdul's three-roomed house is also home to the families of his four sons.

Abdul joins the many Moslems who worship regularly at the mosque.

I have no medical degree but I've acquired a huge amount of experience. All types of people come to me, rich and poor. But the poor more often, as they can't afford a modern doctor and medicines, and sometimes don't want to go to hospital either. I don't have any fixed fee. If the person is poor, I charge very little. If I see he's rich, I ask for more. I earn about Rs. 200 a month. It's not enough, but my sons help.

I mustn't forget to tell you that hospitals in India treat patients who earn under Rs. 500 free of charge. But you have to stand in a long queue, I am told, and most people don't have so much time.

I have no faith in modern medicines, capsules, tablets and such things. I cure by using the right kind of herbs and oils and natural products like turmeric. To give you a simple example, I treat deep cuts and wounds by applying turmeric powder mixed with mustard oil.

Similarly, like lots of other Indians, particularly villagers, I don't use a toothbrush or toothpaste. Instead, I use a *neem* twig or salt or coal to clean my teeth. Yes, I've still got eighteen teeth left even though I'm so old.

I'm happy that at least one of my sons has learnt the traditional medical skill from me. Medicine in India is very old. The Indian medical system started around 2000 B.C. Surgery and difficult brain operations were known in India as early as 500 B.C. This I learnt from a text book on ancient Indian medicine. I can read and write Urdu, Hindi, and a bit of English.

Today, a number of systems are being practised in India side by side – traditional Indian, modern medicine, homeopathy, nature cure. We also have some excellent hospitals, I'm told.

Smallpox was once a great killer but is rare now. Otherwise, the fight continues against malaria – there are lots of mosquitoes in India, you know – cholera, leprosy, tuberculosis, V.D. and cancer.

'Till a year ago I had never seen a train'

Janu Mahdu Kurkutay is a 45-year-old tribal headman of Bapu Gaon in Maharashtra. He has two wives, Parvati and Tulsi, and six children. They live in a thatched hut in the middle of a thick forest, working in their paddy fields and hunting.

Till a year ago, I'd never seen a train or a city or so many people wearing clothes. Then, I was taken to New Delhi to take part in the Republic Day Parade on 26th January. So I'm wiser now and spend many evenings telling whoever calls about the wonders of the city. But I don't think the visit to our capital has changed my way of life.

It is festival time, and one of the headman's sons calls people to dance by playing the tarpa.

We are *Adivasis*, you know. I was told at New Delhi that there are about 25 million of us spread all over India. And – would you believe it? – I actually met some of the other tribes. Of course, they all spoke their own language, but I was able to gather that life is much the same for all of us.

Normally, we don't wear clothes. Our women do put on a little clothing on special occasions, just as we men wear a *langoti*.

We stay with our parents even after we're married and have our own children. There are a few cases where the sons set up separate homes, but this happens mostly when some serious quarrel takes place.

Like other tribal families, we divide the work between ourselves. For the four monsoon months, my father, who is sixty-five years old, my three sons and I remain busy with cultivation, mostly of paddy. This means a lot of work, ploughing, planting and fencing the field.

My wives, Parvati and Tulsi, and my

three daughters grind the grain and bring water from the well – it's quite far off. They also collect dry wood from the forest and exchange it at the weekly market for grain or something else. Sometimes, they help us in the fields, just as we sometimes help them to fetch water.

In our tribal society, we can marry as many times as we want to. It all depends on how many wives one can feed. A priest and the village elders perform the marriage ceremony.

Food is a real problem with us. I must admit that we have gone hungry on more than one occasion. During the monsoons, the rains sometimes fail and there's drought. Some years it rains so hard that our crops are washed away.

When we do have grain, we bake pancakes and prepare gruel. Otherwise, we eat berries and leaves from the forest, and if we're lucky, kill some rabbits or birds. Vegetables? We don't grow any, except potatoes. Money? What would we do with money? Our marketing is based on the barter system. But of late, the younger children, especially my son Madhu, have been persuading us to sell peacock feathers, our wood carvings and the mats that we weave to outside traders for money. The world is changing, he keeps on telling me.

When I think it over, there's some truth in his words. We didn't know what school was till the Government opened up this *ashram* nearby. Some of us send our children so that they can at least get a good meal.

But I for one prefer my own life. I like festival time the best, as do my wives. I hope they don't overhear, but at such times they show off their beads and ornaments. We celebrate the beginning of the monsoons, the season of harvesting and other occasions like births and weddings. There's lots of wild dancing and drinking of liquor made from *mohwa* flowers.

We issue invitations either by beating a drum, or by playing on the *tarpa*, a musical instrument we make from gourds. Whoever hears the music comes and begins to dance. Another joins him. Then another. Soon there are a number of men, women and children, all dancing and swaying together. It's great fun – you must come and join us sometime.

Villagers have traditionally bartered their goods, but now they sell what they weave.

'The weather gods have been kind to me'

***Chowdhry* Narendar Singh, 54, is a farmer in Badripur. His wife, Dulari, helps him to look after the 2-acre (0.8 hectare) farm. They have three children.**

This has been a fine season for me. Look, there in the distance you can see my sugar-cane fields ready for harvesting.

My fields weren't always green and smiling like this. Today, our farm has an ample supply of water from wells, so I can expect good crops. But there was a time not very long ago when I had to rely completely on the rains, as farmers still do in many parts of the country. Of course, a lot still depends on the weather.

The weather gods have been kind to me, but the other day a farmer friend of mine had come from down south and he had a lot of complaints.

'Something or other is always happening,' he said. 'Sometimes it's too little rain and everything dries up. Other times there are floods and all my labour is washed away. Some years it's a cyclone; other years it's a tornado. Sometimes there are locusts. Nature seems always to be at war with us.'

What he said is right to a large extent. But then I say: look at the brighter side. In spite of so many hardships, production has increased remarkably. Take the case of sugar-cane. Compared with ten years ago, today we produce more than three times the amount.

Modern farmers use tractors as well as bullocks for ploughing.

You'll find this increase in all the crops – wheat, rice, maize, pulses, cotton, potatoes, vegetables, fruits, poultry products, tea, coffee and milk production, too. Then how is it that almost seventy per cent of my countrymen are poor and don't even get two good meals a day?

Ah, that's the sad part. Our population seems to grow much faster than our production. Don't forget that after China we're the world's second most populous country. Feeding more than 660 million people is no joke.

Still, I say hats off to our government and agricultural scientists. Now we have high-yielding varieties of seeds, better fertilizers, special TV programmes for farmers. And the government is trying its best to persuade each family to have only two or three children, instead of the six or nine or more that rural families and the uneducated usually have.

Quite honestly, my wife and I feel that family planning is the answer to all our country's problems. We ourselves have only three children and we're a very happy family. We spend most weekdays at the farmhouse. We have to see that the farm labourers – two permanent servants and thirty part-time labourers – do the work properly. Nowadays, we use bullocks as well as the modern tractor for ploughing.

Our children stay in a rented flat in town. It makes it easier for them to attend college. You see, they don't want to farm. My elder son, Ravindra, wants to do computer programming. The younger one wants to become a geologist. And my daughter wants to teach in a school. My wife and I encourage them, as it would be nice to see somebody in the family breaking away from the tradition of full-time farming.

Sundays we all get together either at the farm or in our town flat. We exchange news and views over a good meal – *pulao* and *raita* followed by lots of fruit: mangos or lichis or oranges or guavas – whatever's in season. We keep a buffalo at the farm, so we get our own milk. Buffaloes' milk is quite delicious. Most people here prefer buffaloes' milk to cows' milk. Until a few years ago, we didn't eat onions or garlic. Most of our relatives still don't eat onions.

My earnings vary. Last year, I made a profit of about Rs. 25,000. It's more than enough for our family. But, as I said, the gods have been kind to me. Not all farmers – more than three-quarters of my countrymen are engaged in agriculture – have it so good.

A scene of village life in Badripur.

'Most of my 500 trainees are aged between 5 and 15'

Guru Hanuman is an 81-year-old wrestling coach. He is named after Hanuman, the much revered monkey God of the Hindus. Guru Hanuman runs a wrestling gymnasium or *vyamshala* in the old part of New Delhi.

I can see that you're taken aback. You didn't really expect an eighty-one year old to be active, did you? But I really do believe that a *sewak*, or one who serves, never gets old. I've dedicated my life to the service of wrestling, and I shall continue till I have no more energy – perhaps till I'm ninety or even 100 years old.

I myself took to wrestling when I was seven. Long before that, when I was just a year old, my parents had died in the great plague in Rajasthan, India's desert state. Those were bad times. Relatives looked after me as best they could. But because I was very small and thin, the neighbourhood boys would bully and beat me. So I decided to become a wrestler.

Finding a *guru* or teacher wasn't too difficult. You see, wrestling is an ancient skill in India. Then, as now, most villages had their own *akharas*, or mud pits, for wrestling. It's funny how things change.

Seventy years ago, nobody in India, except the princes and nawabs, played games like cricket, hockey, football or tennis. These were introduced by the British. Instead, we had our own sports like wrestling, *kabaddi*, *kho-kho*, archery and chess. Of course, we had polo, too, but this again could be played only by the very rich.

These days, I've noticed that, by and large, boys and girls in the cities have cricket or football or tennis heroes. Everybody wants to become a Sunil Gavaskar or a Dennis Lillee or a Bjorn

Two of the Guru's young pupils practise their sport in the mud pit.

Borg. But in the villages the young have stuck to their own games. With them, the wrestling heroes of Indian folklore, like Bhim, Angad, Gama and Goonga, are still popular. Most rural youths want to become a Bhim or an Angad.

You want to know what happened after I began my wrestling career? I soon found that besides wrestling training, the *akharas* provided very valuable education. There were rich boys as well as poor boys. We were taught how important it was to help each other and live simply and with honour in society. It was a big change from life as I had known it, for in the *akhara* it didn't matter if one was a high-class *Brahmin* or a low-class *bhangi*.

Today, I run my *vyamshala* on the same lines that I was taught. My day begins at 4.00 a.m., be it summer or winter. I wake up each of my 500 trainees personally. Most are in the age group of five to fifteen years. The eldest is twenty-six years old. They sleep on the bare floor, only a few on *charpoys*. Upon waking, they all come one by one to touch my feet and receive my blessing. This is an old Indian custom. We set a lot of store in respecting our elders and *gurus*, and touch their feet as a mark of respect.

Anyway, we have a quick wash and a massage session, and then we're off – racing, doing various exercises, lifting weights, climbing ropes. At 9.00 a.m., everybody has almonds, apple and orange juice and a little later, milk with lots of cream and *ghee*. Food, lodging and training are all given free. Patrons meet the entire cost.

My boys attend the school next door till lunch time. Back from school, they prepare lunch. I insist on vegetarian

A picture of Hanuman, the monkey-god, after whom the Guru was named.

meals, rich in protein. We provide them with the raw vegetables, *dal*, curd, flour and rice. But the boys do all the cooking, cleaning and washing themselves – it teaches them to be self reliant.

After lunch and a brief rest, it's practice in the mud pits till 9.00 p.m. We do have our own modern foam wrestling mat. It cost us Rs.1,200,000 and is one of only three in the country. But we allow only advanced trainees to practise on it. I'm extremely strict about discipline, diet and daily practice.

I started this *vyamshala* fifty-three years ago. But it was only in 1960 that one of my boys was sent for the first time to the Olympics, in Rome. Since then, a number of my disciples have won gold and other medals at international meets.

But I must stress that winning medals is not everything. I'm satisfied that, even if wrestling fame does not come their way, my boys would at least benefit by becoming educated and able-bodied. Most of them are from rural areas.

I travel a lot both in my own country and to other countries to study the latest training programmes. I can't speak or understand English – Hindi is all I know – so I have to take along an interpreter. There isn't time to do much else as I have my hands full with 500 wrestlers.

'We women work as hard as the menfolk'

Phulki has been roaming from village to village in her cart ever since she was born. She is a blacksmith and designs tools and implements for the village people. Her husband, Dhulia, is also a blacksmith.

I'm a roving blacksmith. Once we were the guardians of Chittor fort. But, over four hundred years ago, an ancestor named Sati Aie Lacha cursed us and we had to take to the nomadic way of life.

Then, when the Mughals came to India and captured our fort in the sixteenth century, we took a vow not to return to Chittor fort or live in settled homes, or draw water from a well, or use a candle for light, or sleep on an elevated bed till Chittor was liberated from the Mughals.

Of course, the last Mughal died more than a hundred years ago and Chittor became free much earlier. But we still stick to our vow as we feel that breaking it would bring bad luck to our community. So we continue to move around the countryside, setting up our furnace wherever we park our cart home.

My husband beats the hot iron with a hammer while I blow the furnace. It's no secret that amongst us gudaliya lohars – 6,000 roving blacksmiths – we women work as hard as the menfolk.

We make things like sickles, pickaxes, and mortar pans for weavers, carpenters, farmers and others. We also do repair work. But my day doesn't end here. I have to grind the flour, pick or buy firewood and then cook the food. While I'm

Phulki and her community gather to dance before a wedding ceremony.

The husband makes the tools, while the wife works the furnace.

working, my daughter Dhulki looks after her baby brother, Parthia.

We manage to earn about Rs. 15 a day. This is more than enough, for as you can see for yourself, we don't believe in comfort. Most of our earnings we spend on food – usually *chapatis* and mutton or chicken curry, and boiled eggs with lots of tea and liquid. The rest we spend on buying a few clothes and lots of silver jewellery. I'm crazy about jewellery: I own more than 15 kg (33 lb) of fine silver jewellery.

These past few years, my husband and I have seen a number of changes. Compared with ten years ago, there are many, many more proper roads. Did you say that the Indian road network is one of the largest in the world, stretching for more than 1,200,000 km (745,650 miles)? We wouldn't know, for we can't read or write. In fact, none of us gudaliya lohars have ever seen the inside of a school. Anyway, more roads makes it easier for us to move around and reach more places.

People are no longer so strict about caste. There was a time when a Brahman wouldn't come near us, for we were, and still are, considered outcasts. But if by chance he did, he had to purify himself by having a bath. Now some Brahmins get us to carry out their repair work.

But not all the changes are good, and that's what bothers me. We see more and more people going in for machine tools, and in the cities at least, fewer and fewer people care for our work. It's a question of survival for us, but I and other gudaliya lohars are determined to practise our skill in iron work and carry on with our way of life till the end. Dhulia makes me forget my worries by singing and telling stories of long ago when we were the guardians of Chittor fort.

Today, I'm very excited – my sister-in-law and her family have come in their cart and brought news. My favourite cousin will be getting married at the next full moon. Marriages amongst us are solemnized before the elders. Yes, the elders make all the decisions.

A day before the wedding, we perform a ceremony to please our gods and ancestors; a goat is sacrificed and a grand feast is held. Dancing and singing begin many days before. To be in time for the wedding, Dhulia and I will be moving in a day or so. But we'll be back, maybe in a year's time, maybe in two years' time. Who can tell?

'Do you see how the tiger is kissing me'

Shib Dayal Singh, 44, is the Head Keeper at the New Delhi Zoological Park. He lives with his wife and six children in a three-roomed house in the zoo itself.

My life is one big adventure. I'm very proud to have more than 3,000 animal friends. Come, let me take you first to Moti, a two-year-old white tiger. See how he's kissing me? He doesn't attack me; I've known him since he was a cub, and he remembers that. Tigers are very affectionate and intelligent animals. Just as the peacock is our national bird, the tiger is the national animal. We also gave the world its first white tiger.

I've always loved animals. I joined this Delhi Zoo – it's one of the largest in the world – twenty years ago. We have six other national parks, plus 135 wild life sanctuaries and twenty-four zoological gardens. I've been to most of them. We're a country rich in wild life.

My day here begins at 6.00 a.m. in summer and a little later in winter. My wife gives me a good breakfast, usually milk, bananas and *parathas*, she knows I may not be back for lunch. Then I get on my bicycle and begin the rounds of the 97 hectare (240 acre) zoo, saying hello to each animal, bird and reptile. We keep more than 1,500 species, and I have to see that each animal is well fed and in good health and that visitors to the zoo don't tease them.

I don't work alone. There are sixty keepers who work under me and help me to feed and look after animals. All the animals greet me like an old friend,

Shib Dayal receives a kiss from Moti, the two-year-old white tiger.

except this monkey. He escaped once. I had to chase him all over the zoo and even climb some trees before I could catch him after he had been loose for hours in the hot sun.

On the whole, working at the zoo is very absorbing. But it has its moments of danger too, like the time when a tiger escaped. We had to shoot it in the end. Another time a rhinoceros escaped. And once a black panther almost got out of the zoo. And then seventeen monkeys broke loose. But luckily, I was able to get them safely back each time. Very brave you say? Well, people thought so, though it was all in a day's work for me, but I was given awards for bravery each time.

Most days, I leave the zoo proper when it becomes dark. My house is within the zoo itself, but by the time I reach home, I'm hungry and very tired. My wife has a hot meal ready for me.

I earn Rs. 700 a month and it's not sufficient to support eight people. Why don't I take another job? I'm not a graduate for one thing. Educational qualifications count more than experience here in India. And I'd feel lost without the animals I love.

But let me tell you about my big problem. I have to arrange the marriages of my five daughters. And in our Aggarwal community, we have to bid for a husband. If I want to marry my daughter to a doctor or an engineer, I will have to give at least Rs. 40,000 to the boy's family. Where will I get so much money for each of my daughters? Often, my wife and I can't sleep at nights worrying over this.

Certainly, this dowry system is bad. But what can I do? If I don't give the money, nobody will marry my daughters. It doesn't matter how intelligent or nice or good looking or ugly they are. And I have to marry them to somebody from my own Aggarwal community.

I daren't marry into another community or caste or religion. There's no law against it. In fact, the government and other sensible people advise us to marry outside our community if possible, and not to give a dowry. But it's just that were we to do so, relatives and others from our own community would stop speaking to us.

So you see, I'm very happy with my work. And at home we're a very happy family. But it scares me to think of how I will marry off my daughters.

The Langur monkey is content with his meal of guavas, but he is not always so placid.

'Theatre in India is more than 2000 years old'

Rajinder Nath is a 46-year-old drama director. He lives in a rented, four-roomed flat in New Delhi. He also teaches English in a college of Delhi University.

I was only six years old when I acted in my first play. With the costumes, drums and music, it was so exciting that I decided there and then to specialize in drama. So after college, I attended the National School of Drama for five years.

A scene from a drama based on the historical play of Heer Ranjha.

I don't act in plays any more; I direct dramas, all sorts of plays. And I find it a great experience. You know, till some years ago, very few people came to see our plays. Without an audience, naturally, our plays didn't last for more than two or three shows.

Now we have an audience of about 300 for each show and there is actually a demand for good plays. There was a play which ran for 100 days. But I'm speaking of urban theatre which is professional and has all the modern aids like lighting and sound effects, specially trained actors and good sets. Professional companies, though still few, exist mainly in our large cities.

Theatre in India is more than 2,000 years old. In the olden days, groups of actors used to move around the countryside, giving performances in village streets and courtyards. For centuries, most of our rajahs and nawabs were great patrons of drama. Of course, the themes were mainly religious and dealt with the deeds of our gods.

Even today, if you happen to be in northern India during October or November, you'll find the *Ram Lila* being acted out in every city, town and village. The *Ram Lila* runs continuously for a month. A different scene from the *Ramayana* is enacted every night.

The actors perform on a temporary stage in some open space, with oil lamps providing the light. Entry is free, with everyone sitting in the open on the ground.

At sunset on the last day of the performance, a huge effigy of the many-headed evil God Ravana is burnt. This is known as *Dussehra*; thousands come to watch the burning of Ravana.

Like the *Mahabharata*, the *Ramayana* is a great epic and contains the story of Ram and Sita and their fight against the bad Ravana. In every part of the country, people have their own religious dramas in addition to the *Ramayana* and *Mahabharata*. But in the north, village plays and dance dramas all take their themes from the *Ramayana* and the *Mahabharata*. There are so many, many interesting incidents in them, in which the good always win over the bad.

I don't have time to go to see the *Ram Lila* now. *Ram Lila* performances last till around midnight. But many evenings in October or November, when I drive back from my own rehearsals, I'm tempted to step in. Folk theatre is really doing very well in India.

Rajinder Nath directs the actors in a new production.

'Being rich is not in my stars, so I'm content'

Ramaswami, 35, is a fortune teller from Madras, the capital of Tamil Nadu. A widower, he lives in a rented room with the youngest of his six children.

Once upon a time, I owned some land near Madras and did my own farming. Then the rains failed, as they often do in South India. Because there was no water, my crop of rice dried up and died. Can you imagine, our village didn't even have drinking water?

This doesn't always happen. I was reading in the paper just the other day that out of nearly 550,000 villages in India, more than 490,000 have a good supply of water. I think I was just unlucky to own land in a village which had not yet been provided with water.

Anyway, living from day to day became difficult. I didn't have much money. I was depending on my crops, but the monsoon had let me down. Of course, I and my wife Rati – she was alive then – began looking for work, any work. But the monsoon had ruined thousands of other small farmers like me and they were all desparately looking for work. At last, the day came when I had money left for only one more meal.

It was then that it struck me. Why shouldn't I become a fortune teller? Who doesn't want to know about the future? We Indians particularly believe a lot in luck and fate. I already knew something about astrology and palmistry – my uncle had taught me. Both astrology and palmistry originated in India and are very, very old. My uncle used to tell me that it was from India that astrology and palmistry reached China, Persia and other countries.

Ramaswami is about to release Tota, the parrot, from its cage to pick a card.

Even in these modern times, most people in India carry out important work after they have been to an astrologer for advice. So you see, an astrologer is a very important person in Indian society.

Usually, whenever a new baby is born into a Hindu family, the astrologer has to make out a horoscope for the baby. Besides, it would interest you to know that almost 90 per cent of Hindu marriages are decided by the stars.

Most people don't move into a new house, or start a new business until the time is auspicious. Even some Ministers are sworn in only when the planets are in the right position.

I draw up horoscopes when people ask me to do so. I charge Rs. 10 per horoscope. Most of the time I spend sitting by the roadside with my two parrots, Tota and Toti. I keep a lot of cards with predictions printed on them. When a person wants his fortune told, Tota or Toti hop out of their cage and pick out a prediction card for them. People pay me 50 paise for this parrot fortune service. I also sell birthstones and charms.

I earn about Rs. 300 a month doing this, which is quite enough for my daughter and me and the parrots. Of course, I don't own, and can't even think of owning, a house or furniture or any luxury. A two-band radio is all I own. But we have enough for food, and that's what counts. Not all astrologers are poor like me. Some are very, very rich and live in air-conditioned bungalows and move around in cars. But being rich is not in my stars, so I'm content.

In summer, people stay indoors in the afternoons because of the heat. This leaves my afternoons free to sit under a shady tree and read and study ancient astrological charts. I've learnt to speak and read and write in Hindi, though Tamil is my native tongue. And of course, I know Sanskrit.

Most evenings, I go straight home where my daughter Ishwari has a meal of rice and *sambhar* ready for me. Some evenings I go to the races. Not horse races – those are for the big sahibs in the big cities like Delhi, Calcutta, Bombay and Bangalore. I only go to see and bet on *tonga* races.

Soon, when I've collected enough money, I shall send Ishwari to school. I myself never went to school; there were very few in my time. Ishwari is quite happy as it is, spending the day playing *Chor-chipai* (hide and seek) with the neighbourhood kids or doing embroidery. She misses having a mother.

People don't generally remarry in India. Socially, remarriage is not considered right. In fact, people think it's unlucky to marry a widow or a widower. So I haven't given it a serious thought or looked at my horoscope to see if I will marry again. If it is in my stars, perhaps some day . . .

One of Ramaswami's favourite hobbies is to watch and bet on the tonga races.

'In our films the good guys always beat the bad guys'

Praveen Sood is a 30-year-old film actor. He lives in a two-roomed flat in Bombay, the capital of Maharashtra. His wife Asha looks after the flat and helps him to answer the fan mail.

It's a funny set-up. When I was a boy I was crazy about films and film stars. Now I find that some people are crazy about me. Here in India the public simply idolizes film stars. You know, only about 36 per cent of us Indians can read and write, and turn to books and magazines for knowledge and relaxation. For most people, movies are the only form of relaxation and source of information about fashion, sport, history and the world in general.

The Taj Hotel is one of Bombay's major tourist attractions.

Praveen works with many beautiful actresses; they can fall in love, but they must not kiss.

In the cities, films are advertised on huge colourful posters and in the daily papers. But in towns and villages, just to make sure that everybody knows, three or four men go around beating drums and announcing a new film through loudspeakers. I've signed up for another six films. But, I don't think of myself as a film star – yet. In a country which produces 130 films in Hindi alone every year, six films are good for making a beginning, but not for becoming a star. More films are made in India than any other country. I do believe that becoming a star depends on one's stars.

Most of our films deal with social problems like untouchability, inter-caste marriages, family planning, becoming good mothers-in-law and so on. Then there are religious films, films for children, and, in recent years, a number of thrillers. In our films the good guys always win over the bad guys. I prefer to be a good guy in films with a social theme.

But I must tell you that, by and large, most films are made to a set pattern. The theme has to be set in a love story – but no kissing is allowed. Then there have to lots of songs – at least five or six per film, along with a few dance numbers. And a gun- or fist-fight between the hero and the villain.

My own day-to-day life is very busy, especially when I'm in Bombay. You know, Bombay, Calcutta and Madras are the most important film centres in the country. After the day's shooting at the studios, I race home in my car to pick up my wife. There's usually some gala party laid on.

We usually eat out. Bombay is one of the few cities in India where there's night life. In fact, with its ships and beach, and skyscrapers, its electric trains, fashion houses and discos and bars and the fast pace of life, Bombay reminds me of the West.

An actor can earn between Rs. 10,000 and Rs. 2,000,000 per film. I also own a record shop, so I can afford to live a very luxurious life. But my wife and I have simple tastes. Like thousands of others, my wife and I still like nothing better than to spend the evenings watching a movie with our kids.

A Hindi film runs for about two and a half hours, but every cinema hall in the country has to run a newsreel and a short documentary film before the main film begins. As a form of entertainment, movies are cheap. Tickets range from Rs. 2.00 to Rs. 10.00.

Right now, I'm planning to produce a film myself. It will require a lot of money, certainly, particularly as more and more films are being made in colour. But then look at the export possibilities. Not only does India lead the world in the production of feature films, it also exports them to nearly ninety countries of the world. So if I'm lucky it should turn out to be a worthwhile investment – don't you think so?

'A herd of wild elephants had held up the train'

Dipali Das is a 25-year-old security assistant with the North East Frontier Railway. She lives with her five younger sisters in Gauhati, near Dispur, the capital of Assam State. Because her parents are dead, Dipali has to help her younger sisters through college.

You'll find my life very different from those in other parts of the country. Here in Assam the sun sets early and the night is long. And, for eight months of the year, it rains very hard. Day in and day out we hear nothing but the pitter-patter of raindrops. Cherrapunji in nearby Meghalaya has the highest rainfall not only in India but also in the world.

Naturally, the area around is heavily forested and everything grows by leaps and bounds. With so many flowers and leaves and ferns to choose from, I've become quite a specialist in flower decoration. I like the Japanese style of Ikebana flower arrangement the best.

In my job as a security assistant with the railways, I have to help ensure the safety of the passengers and the goods that we carry.

Assam is a very important region for the supply of oil. Two of India's biggest oil refineries are here at Gauhati and Digboi. But Assam isn't very thickly populated. It's a hilly region and still quite undeveloped. So unlike the rest of India, we have only one main railway line from Calcutta to Gauhati.

Mine is an 8.00 a.m. to 3.00 p.m. job, and so far has consisted mainly of filing work. But I'm not complaining. The pay I get – Rs. 800 – is very useful, especially as my parents are not alive. Rs. 800 is good pay, if one is single, but certainly not enough for a family. But when I think of others who get Rs. 200, or have

An elephant safari. There are many elephants in Assam, most of them wild.

no job at all, I think I'm fortunate.

Besides, my job contains a fair amount of excitement too. A few months ago, a train was overdue. Four hours passed and all of us at the railway station became very nervous. Could somebody have put a bomb on the train? Could it have been derailed?

The train steamed in eight hours late. Guess what had happened. A herd of wild elephants – there are plenty of wild elephants and rhinoceros in Assam – had held up the train. The herd had refused to move from the track despite the train whistle and the passengers' shouts. So the poor driver and passengers could do nothing but wait till the elephants decided to move off. As a result of hold-ups like these, people who are in a hurry and who can afford it, prefer to fly to Gauhati.

Dancing is a way of life with the Assamese, often to the music of a drum.

When I get home from the office, my sisters have a light meal of vegetable noodles or fish and rice ready for me. And a glass of tea. Assam is full of tea plantations and is known as India's Tea State. Our region supplies tea to a large part of the world. The tourists who visit Assam are mainly lovers of nature or wildlife. And they always ask for pineapples – we have lots of them.

I travel a fair bit both in India and abroad. As well as being a security assistant, I'm also a dancer and like giving dance performances. My favourites are the traditional dances of Assam like *Bihu*, which is a spring dance. I practise dancing every day for at least one hour and also teach dancing.

Most Assamese are expert dancers, for dancing is a way of life with us. Partly because it gives us an opportunity to get together. This is quite natural as there isn't much else by way of entertainment here. Hardly any movie houses for instance. I mustn't forget to tell you that as in most parts of India, here in Assam too, we dance for the gods, like the *Devadasi* dance, which is performed by female dancers in the *Siva* and *Vaishnava* temples of Assam.

Recently, I've also danced in the film *Shree Shree Ma Kamakhya*. The film is in Assamese, but I can also speak English besides Bengali and a little Hindi. I wish I had more time to learn some more languages and do some embroidery and jute weaving at which my sisters and other Assamese women are very good.

At present, however, I'm not sure whether I'll be able to stay here for long. You see I've had invitations from various parts of the country to teach the dances of Assam to students from other states. The trouble is that I love my home and don't really want to leave, so I'm still sitting on the offer.

'We Sikhs are not allowed to cut our hair'

Jasbir Singh Kaith is a 32-year-old tailor in Jullunder. With his wife and three children they share a four-roomed flat with seven other relatives.

Lots of people depend on me. Just the other day, my morning began with a lady who wanted me to stitch a silk blouse. She said: 'Tailor, please have it ready by tomorrow evening, otherwise I won't be able to attend this party.' Then another lady came in with dress material. Then another, and another. And so it goes on the whole day. I get at least ten new customers per day.

Of course, this means a lot of new business, but it also means back-breaking work for me. Often, I and my eight workers have to work far into the night to complete the orders. I know that if I didn't have the clothes ready on time, my customers would be very disappointed.

I make mainly traditional Indian dresses for ladies, but also Western jeans and jackets. I don't stitch clothes for men, but I can tell you what they wear.

In cities and towns, most men wear Western type shirts and pants and jeans. Naturally, socks and shoes also. In winter, they add pullovers and stylish coats. But in the rural areas, most men wear only cotton shirts and *dhotis* in summer. No socks or shoes, only sandals. In winter, they wrap a woollen shawl round themselves.

Jasbir takes his family shopping.

In recent years I've noticed that a lot of synthetic cloth has come on the market.

But it is so expensive that only the rich and middle class can afford it. Anyway, most people, rich and poor alike, still prefer cotton. That's natural, for cotton clothes are just right for our hot climate.

Cotton is very cheap, too. Some people tell me that they feel patriotic wearing cotton, as most of it is grown in India. I'm not fond of clothes myself.

I didn't want to become a tailor. I wanted to join the army. But my father – he's seventy years old now – was a tailor. When he fell ill, somebody had to take over the business and earn for the family, and have enough money to arrange the marriage of my four sisters. So, since I was the eldest, I had to give up my studies and take over the business.

I earn about Rs. 2,000 a month from my tailoring shop. Together with the Rs. 1,500 that my brother earns (he's also a tailor, though we work separately), we manage our joint family comfortably. We're Sikhs, you know, followers of a fifteenth-century reformer known as Guru Nanak. We speak Punjabi at home but I can also speak Hindi and English.

I hardly ever get time to be away from my shop. The public keeps us tailors busy all the year round – there are at least five or six of us in each locality. I used to love playing and watching football. But now, where's the time? On Saturdays, I take an hour off to escort my wife and children to the market. You know, times are changing, but my family, at least, doesn't like the idea of a lady going out alone.

Though I have to work, Sunday is my big day. It's on Sundays that my wife makes my favourite *Makki ki roti* and *saag*. It's also on Sundays that I wash my long hair. We Sikhs aren't allowed to cut our hair, you see. So we tie it in a knot on top of our head and wrap a turban round it. It makes it easy to spot us, doesn't it?

So far, I've only been as far as Amritsar, on a pilgrimage to the Golden Temple – the main pilgrimage centre for us Sikhs. Someday, I'd love to travel all over India. My wife Kanwaljit deserves a change, too. She does all the cooking and knitting and housework for us, besides helping with the elder children's homework. So next year, if you happen to come this way, you might find that I'm on holiday after all.

The Golden Temple of Amritsar, the main pilgrimage centre for Sikhs.

'We eat sitting cross-legged on the floor'

Atma Ram is a 49-year-old potter in Dehra Dun. He and his wife and six children live with his mother in a three-roomed dwelling which Atma built with his own hands in the town's Potter Colony.

It's hard work from 7.00 a.m. to 6.00 p.m., especially under the hot Indian summer sun. But then you know, I'm self-employed, and if I don't put in all my efforts, I know my large family will go hungry.

I begin the day by mixing clay and then start shaping it with my hands on the potter's wheel. Like my father and grandfather before me, I make clay toys, flower pots, water jars, utensils and many other things. In all, I turn out about 600 articles a day. But then, on rainy days, and in the monsoon months of July, August and September, when it rains and rains, I just cannot work.

I work in the open courtyard outside my house. Lots of people come to see me working and admire and buy the things I've made. They think I'm a wizard, and that making things by hand is a grand life.

But they don't know how difficult it can be. I and other potters like me usually don't even take a break for lunch. That's mainly because, in our very hot climate, if we take a heavy meal in the afternoon, we feel like going to sleep.

But my wife Bina Devi gives me and the children a really great meal in the morning. Boiled rice, *dal* with fried onions, curried vegetables, generally

Atma Ram is helped by his wife and children as he works at his wheel in his courtyard.

cauliflower, cabbage, potatoes or peas with lots of chillies and spices, and *chapatis*. Then lots of tea. And soon afterwards, tobacco for me, which I smoke in a hookah or waterpipe. As you can guess, for cooking and eating, we make our own utensils. We never use spoons, for we always eat our food with our hands, while sitting cross-legged on the floor.

In the evening, I finish work when the sun sets. Before going into the house, I count the money I've made. I earn between Rs. 30 and 40 a day. With so many children and their schooling to look after, this money is not always enough. But then I'm happy in my work and it's the only thing I can do really well. There were very few schools when I was young, you see, so I can't read or write.

Still, I learnt a lot of stories and songs from my parents, and I can play a drum and the flute. When it gets dark, and we all gather round the fire for our dinner, my children and my wife want me to tell them about life. It's a good way to relax, and we like it better than going out to some fair or late-night movie.

My children like most to hear about the days when our settlement had no water or electricity, and we had to hire horses to fetch clay from the river bed. We used to be scared of meeting dacoits on the lonely riverside.

Of course, all that has changed, you know. Now we have water and electricity and a truck brings the clay for us. But with these changes for the better, new problems have beset us. I and other potters have to work extra hard and think of new designs to keep up with the competition from modern steel and factory goods.

Today there are about 1,500,000 of us.

Bina Devi takes the wares for sale from house to house on her head.

But let me tell you my secret. Seeing so many machines and factories going up all over the place sometimes sets me wondering. When my sons finish school and grow up, will they also become skilled potters, or will they take up some other job?

When my wife sees me sad like this, she tells me not to worry. If the children become potters, good, they will keep up the work our family has been doing for ages. And if they take up a modern job, still good, for they'll be able to afford better things that we don't have, like an electric fan or a television set.

'It does feel nice to be recognized wherever you go'

Salma Sultan is a young newsreader with the Delhi TV Centre. Salma and her family live with her sister and her household. The joint family of seven live in a four-bedroomed house. They have five servants.

When they meet me, people often say: 'Gosh, Salma, what a glamorous job you've got.' There is some glamour, and it does feel nice to be recognized wherever you go. But most of the time it's solid work. I've been with Delhi TV for more than ten years now. I read the Hindi news and do some other programmes as well.

Working in TV in India is a very challenging job. Over six million people live in New Delhi, the capital. Some of these people are South Indians, some Bengalis, some Punjabis, Gujeratis and Garwhalis; some are Hindus, some are Muslims, some Parsis and some Christians. They are an endless variety from all the thirty-one states and territories of the country. You'll find this same mixture all over India.

They're all Indians, of course, and they do have a lot of things in common. But not only are their mother tongues different, they also have different habits, customs and festivals. So you see how difficult it becomes for me and others at the TV centre to have something of interest for everybody. We only have one TV channel at the moment, and we don't have colour TV yet.

There are eighteen TV centres in the country so far. It takes time to spread a TV network over 3,287,606 square kilometres (1,269,346 square miles) – which is the area of our country, the seventh largest in the world.

In any case, TV in India is still quite new. Our centre at Delhi was set up in 1959, but the other centres were all constructed in the last ten years. Actually, TV is a big draw here, as almost 64 per cent of our people can't read or write. So they educate themselves by listening to radio and watching TV programmes.

Not everyone owns a TV set, by any means. The cheapest set costs about Rs. 2,000, and a lot of people can't afford them. Realizing this, the government has presented TV sets to a number of villages.

But despite the cost, over the last few years I've seen more and more people

Both Salma and her husband love food. Delhi offers them a large variety.

buying TV sets. It's become something of a status symbol, like owning a scooter or a refrigerator. Those who don't have their own sets simply drop in at a neighbour's to watch TV, especially the Hindi film shown on Sundays. Neighbours don't seem to mind. In fact, they welcome visitors – it's an old Indian tradition never to turn away a visitor, or a beggar.

School lessons are telecast every morning on weekdays. Ordinary TV transmission begins at 6.00 every evening and lasts till 10.00. This leaves me just enough time to do research for TV programmes. At home, I'm very fond of arranging flowers. But the main household tasks like cleaning, cooking and serving we leave to the servants.

Both my husband and I have a liking for Chinese and Mughlai food. Of late, we've been going to restaurants pretty often. Some very good eating places have opened in Delhi in the last few years.

The car parked in the driveway is a Mercedes. We use it when the whole family has to go out. Otherwise, we use the smaller, Indian-made Fiat. Of course it's expensive, because petrol prices are rising. But having one's own transport saves a lot of time, Delhi being a very large city.

Between the two of us, my husband and I earn about Rs. 5,000 a month, sufficient to lead a fairly comfortable life. So far, my sister's family and our family live as a joint family. Now my husband and I have decided to move, and we're looking out for a house. Living as a joint family is a very good arrangement. It's just that we've been married ten years and think it's high time we had a place of our own.

What little time I can spare from my job and family, I like to spend with friends, or just listening to music. Personally, I believe in God – I'm a Muslim you know – and I'm thankful for the full and busy life that I lead.

The national celebrations of Republic Day are always afforded special coverage on TV.

'There are about 800 daily papers in India'

K. Ramakrishnan, 55, is from the coastal region of Kerala. He is the editor of a magazine for children.

You've met me at a very happy time in my life. You see, I got married just six months ago. Yes, it's unusual for a person in India to wed so late. Because so much importance is attached to it, most people here get married by the time they're twenty-five – or thirty at the latest.

But somehow I led such a rich, full life that I never gave marriage a serious thought – until, of course, I met Anandavalli. Our wedding was quite unusual; it was a marriage of choice, not an arranged marriage.

By and large, weddings in India are arranged by parents and relatives. No, no, I'm not talking of the actual arrangements for the big day. I mean it's the parents who select a marriage partner for their children. Haven't you seen the pages and pages of matrimonial advertisements in the newspapers?

There are somewhere around 12,000 newspapers in Hindi, English and regional languages in India. Of these, about 800 are daily papers. Most are owned by individuals and various companies. The Government owns very few of the papers – hardly 3 per cent of them. Nearly a third of our papers are published from the four metropolitan cities of Delhi, Bombay, Calcutta and Madras.

The people of Kerala love flowers. This lady sells flowers from house to house.

I've been in and out of the newspaper and publishing trade for twenty-seven years now, and I've seen a lot of changes. These days, there's a lot of competition amongst publications. I think it's a very healthy sign. Another thing that I've noticed: as compared with, say, ten years ago, more women and girls are going in for journalism and making a mighty good job of it too.

We're one of the leading book publishing countries in the world today, bringing out more than 15,000 titles every year. We export books to about eighty countries.

I for one really love books and magazines. At home, my wife and I spend a major part of the evening reading. Of course, between ourselves we talk in Malayalam, our native tongue, but we prefer to read English.

The magazine I edit is an English-language magazine for children, and contains a little bit of everything. The folk tales that we publish are very popular. Indian culture has a huge store of folk tales and stories, you know – literally thousands.

Every Sunday, I hold discussions with children on what they would like to read. And I must tell you how pleased I am. Twenty-five years ago, hardly 35 per cent of our country's children could read or write. Today, almost 86 per cent of them attend school. By the way, I must tell you that in the whole of India, my state of Kerala has the highest number of literate people – more than 60 per cent.

My day begins early. The milkman comes at 5.30 a.m. Then comes the flower-woman selling flowers. A lot of people here in India buy flowers to make an offering to the gods. Yes, my wife and I do *puja* every morning and sing

Palm trees line the coast of Kerala, which is famous for its coconuts.

bhajans (religious songs).

Before I catch a bus for the office, my wife packs lunch for me. Before that, she gives me a really nice breakfast with lots of milk and coffee and coconuts – Kerala coconuts are famous everywhere.

I hurry back from the office at 5.00 p.m. as I know my wife will be waiting. I change from my shirt and pants into a fresh shirt and *mundu*, the traditional Kerala dress. As I told you, my wife and I read most evenings. Sometimes we go out to plays or art exhibitions or music recitals.

Once in a while, we watch a Kathakali performance. It's a dance drama in which gods and demons and ogres march across the stage, wearing clothes that are truly awe-inspiring.

'Only one-third of our villages possess electricity'

Hira Lal Tayal is a 29-year-old engineer in Mathura, the birthplace of Lord Krishna. He and his wife share his earnings and his four-roomed rented house with his aged parents and two younger brothers.

I've wanted to be an engineer ever since I was in school. Partly because the pay – Rs. 1,500 a month at that time – seemed good, as I belonged to a poor family. Partly because, even then, engineers were in great demand in the country.

Today I have no money problems and on the Rs. 2,000 a month salary that I get from the National Thermal Power Corporation, I can keep my family in comfort. I own a refrigerator, TV, and a scooter, just like other middle-class families. Besides, my job, which is concerned

The Bhakra Nangal Dam, India's largest multi-purpose dam.

with making power available to the country, keeps me on my toes.

What do I mean by power? I'm talking of electric power, thermal power, nuclear power and so on. As a country, I feel we're very fortunate to have more than twenty large rivers. As you know, the Ganga, or Ganges, is not only the holiest river in the land, its also the most useful.

On these rivers we've set up twenty-eight large dams and we're planning many more. The dams supply water for irrigation, control floods and also provide power. The Bhakra Nangal Dam is India's biggest multi-purpose river valley scheme so far.

When I look back over the years, I feel good. We've come a long way since the country's first hydro-electric power-station was set up in 1900. In addition to so many hydro-electric projects, thermal stations now supply almost 60 per cent of electricity to the country. And since 1969, the nuclear power-station at Tarapur has also been functioning.

Our industries alone use almost 65 per cent of the electricity. But it saddens me to think that only about 35 per cent of our villages possess electricity, while the others have to make do with traditional oil lamps, lanterns and candles. It takes time in a vast country like ours. These days, I'm very actively involved in the construction of four World-Bank-aided thermal power-stations.

It's when I'm travelling – and I often have to go on inspection tours – that my problems begin. I've toured almost the whole of India, and some other Asian countries. For one thing, I'm a pure vegetarian – no eggs, no meat. Not only that, I'm not a Jain but like the Jains I don't eat food which contains onions or garlic.

It's just my luck, but fried onions and garlic form the base of most Indian curries and are usually added to vegetables even when they are cooked dry. So when I'm out, I'm reduced to eating plain curd and *chapatis* or rice or sometimes just fruit alone.

There's also a big language problem. People in different parts of the country speak about 1,652 different dialects and languages. People in Bengal talk largely in Bengali. In Assam its Assamese. In South India its Tamil or Telegu or Malayalam. In Goa its Konkani or Portuguese. And so it differs in every part and in each of the thirty-one states and territories of India.

I only know Hindi and English. Most urban and middle and upper class people can understand, read and talk fluently in English – with an Oxford accent at that. But the labouring classes, the tribals and the poor people – who form almost 70 per cent of the total population – don't know any English. So you see how difficult it can become for us to communicate with each other. At such times, I wish I were a linguist instead of an engineer.

Hira Lal often exists on a diet of only fruit. Mangoes are a particular favourite.

Facts

Capital city: New Delhi.
Principal language: Hindi is the official language. English is used for many official purposes. About 16 regional languages are also recognized in the constitution, and many others are spoken.
Currency: Indian rupee = 100 paise, and is worth about 6p or 3 U.S. cents.
Religion: The religious breakdown of the population (1971 census): Hindi – 82.7 per cent; Moslem – 11.21 per cent; Christian – 2.6 per cent; Sikh – 1.89 per cent; Buddhist – 0.7 per cent; Jain – 0.47 per cent.
Population: 711,660,000 (1982 estimate). The population increases each month by 1 million. India is the seventh largest and second most populous country in the world. The most heavily populated areas are those surrounding the Ganges valley, and the southern states of Kerala and Tamil Nadu. The government has encouraged the growth of medium-sized cities and towns. In 1971 42 per cent of the population were 14 years old and younger, and only 5.2 per cent were over 60 years old. Many births are unregistered and there is a high rate of infant mortality.
Climate: The climate ranges from temperate to tropical. Heavy monsoons in June and July. Rainfall varies widely. There are 3 main climatic regions: The Deccan Plateau (center and south); the Himalayas; the Indo-Gangetic plain. People tend to go to the hill resorts during the very hot summers.
Government: India is a federal republic and has the longest written constitution of all countries in the world. Legislative power is vested in Parliament, which has: a President, who is the constitutional Head of State, elected for 5 years by an electoral college; two houses – Council of States with not more than 250 members, of which some are indirectly elected by the State Assemblies for 6 years and some are nominated by the President for 6 years; House of the People, which has 544 members, elected by universal adult suffrage for 5 years. There are 22 self-governing states, each with a Governor appointed by the President for 5 years and a Council of Ministers. There are also 9 Union Territories, administered by the President through an administrator. There are 32 municipal corporations; 1,493 municipalities; 249 town area committees; 202 notified area committees; and 62 cantonment boards.
Education: Education is primarily the responsibility of individual state governments, though in Union Territories responsibility lies with central government. Elementary education to the age of 14 years is theoretically compulsory in all states except 2. Lower primary education (6 to 11 years) is free; upper primary education (11 to 14 years) is free in 12 states. The government aims to provide 10 years' general school education and 2 years' higher secondary education, with free, compulsory education to the age of 14 years. There are also schools for professional, technical and craft subjects. Adult education is being afforded high priority. In 1971 only 34.5 per cent of the population was literate. India has 118 universities and 4,569 colleges.
Housing: A major problem. In many houses the average number of persons is 3–4 to a room. In rural areas about 94 per cent and in urban areas about 46 per cent of families own their homes. Rural houses are mostly of mud. There is much inadequate accommodation in cities – due to increasing population and the movement from country to town. There is a scarcity of land for development and of building materials.
Agriculture: Agriculture is the chief industry of India. About 70 per cent of the people depend on the land for their living. It accounts for almost half the national income. Main crops are: cardamom – India supplies 70 per cent of world consumption; rice – most important food-grain crop; wheat – second most important food-grain crop; groundnuts; rape seed; and mustard; sesame seed; linseed; cotton seed; coffee; sugarcane; cotton; jute; tea; natural rubber; livestock; and opium poppy cultivated under licence. Crops are often damaged by drought and floods. Increasing use of irrigation and chemical fertiliz-

ers. A large percentage of farms are concentrated on a very small percentage of total area under cultivation. India has the fourth largest coal reserves in the world and largely untapped fishing and forestry resources.
Industry: Bombay has 45 per cent of the industry of the state of Maharashtra, which in turn has 20 per cent of the industry of the whole country. India ranks among the top 10 industrial nations of the world and is the most highly industrialized country in S. and SE. Asia. New industries (heavy engineering, iron and steel, chemicals and electronics) have expanded rapidly.
The media: Radio is controlled by the Ministry of Information and Broadcasting. News Service Division of All India Radio (AIR) is one of the largest news organizations in the world. By 1978 15 per cent of the population could receive television broadcasts. TV controlled by Ministry of Information and Broadcasting. The government instals and maintains radio and TV sets in community centres as means of publicity and propaganda. There is no national press. Recently-imposed censorship has been relaxed. Because of many languages spoken, English-language press essential.

Glossary

Adivasi A member of a tribe, usually living in a forest.
ashram A place of rest and study.
bhajan A religious song.
bhangi A sweeper.
Brahman A member of the highest or priestly caste in the Hindu caste system.
caste Any of the four major hereditary classes, the Brahman, Kshatriya, Vaisya and Sudra, into which Hindu society is divided.
charpoy A wooden cot woven with thick jute strings.
chowdhry Respected landowner of long standing.
dacoit A member of a gang of armed robbers.
dal Pulses, a common foodstuff in India.
guru Hindu or Sikh religious teacher or leader, giving personal spiritual guidance to his disciples.
Jain A follower of Mahavira, a religious leader during the sixth century B.C.
kutchery Law court.
langoti A loincloth.
Pandit A priest or one who is learned in the Vedas.
Raj Kumar A prince.
Rupee The Indian unit of currency (see 'India Facts' for its value).
tonga A small, roofed carriage drawn by a horse.
Veda Any or all of the most ancient sacred writings of Hinduism.
Vishnava Devotees of the god Vishnu.